Atlanta, GA

It's old
with lots of new!

It's big
but friendly, too!

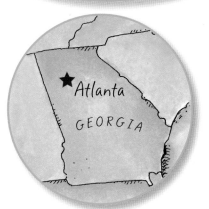

Atlanta
GEORGIA

The places where you live and visit help shape who you become. So find out all you can about the special places around you!

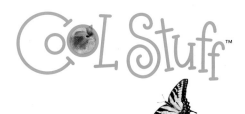

Cool Stuff™

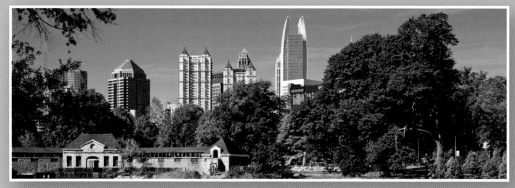

The Atlanta skyline through city park trees.

CREDITS

Series Concept and Development
Kate Boehm Jerome

Design
Steve Curtis Design, Inc. (www.SCDchicago.com), Roger Radke, Todd Nossek

Reviewers and Contributors
Sarah Solomon, Public Relations Specialist, Atlanta Convention and Visitors Bureau; Lisa A. Boehm, writer and editor; Eric Nyquist, researcher; Mary L. Heaton, copy editor

Photography
Cover(a), Back Cover(a), i(a) © Yasonya/Shutterstock; Cover(b), Back Cover(b), i(b) © Leighton Photography & Imaging/Shutterstock; Cover(c), vi(b) © David Lee/Shutterstock; Cover(d) © Rosetta-hidek/Shutterstock; Cover(e), ix(d), xi(b), xvi(b), xvi(h) © iofoto/Shutterstock; ii(a), xvi(f) © Darryl Brooks/Shutterstock; iii(a), viii(b), xvi(c) © zimmytws/Shutterstock; iv(a) © Judy Kennamer/Shutterstock; v(a) © 2009 The Jim Henson Company™/Courtesy Center for Puppetry Arts; vi(a), xvi(d) © Lars Lindblad/Shutterstock; vii(a) © 2007, Kevin C. Rose/AtlantaPhotos.com; vii(b) © Torian/Shutterstock; viii(a) © jackweichen_gatech/Shutterstock; viii(c) Courtesy CityPass; ix(a) © Mike Liu/Shutterstock; ix(b) © Joseph Becker/ Shutterstock; ix(c), xvi(g) Courtesy Stone Mountain Park; x(a) By TheCustomOfLife/Wikimedia; xi(a) stocksnapp/Shutterstock; xii(a) Courtesy Underground Atlanta; xii(b) By Gray wolf/Wikimedia; xiii(a) © Michael Portman; xiii(b) © Mark Winfrey/Shutterstock; xiv(a) © L. Prang & Co., Boston/Courtesy Library of Congress; xv(a) Courtesy the Kenan Research Center, Atlanta History Center; xv(b) © Courtesy Richard Weisser/ RichardWeisser.com; xvi(a) © Weldon Schloneger/Shutterstock; xvi(e) © Christopher Meder-Photography/Shutterstock

Illustration
i © Jennifer Thermes/Photodisc/Getty Images

ISBN 978-1-4396-0062-7
Library of Congress Catalog Card Number: 2009943368

Published by Arcadia Publishing
Charleston SC, Chicago IL, Portsmouth NH, San Francisco CA

For all general information contact Arcadia Publishing at:
Telephone   843-853-2070
Fax   843-853-0044
Email   sales@arcadiapublishing.com
For Customer Service and Orders:
Toll-Free   1-888-313-2665

Visit us on the Internet at www.arcadiapublishing.com

Contents

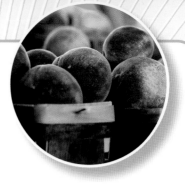

Atlanta

Georgia

Spotlight on Atlanta!

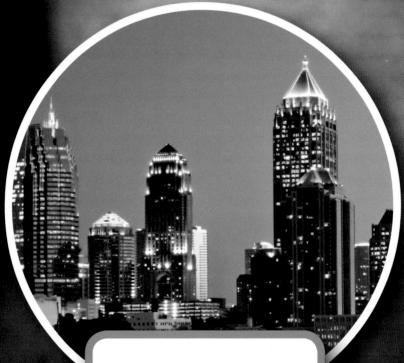

A tlanta is the capital of Georgia—it's also the largest city in the state!

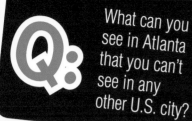 **Q:** What can you see in Atlanta that you can't see in any other U.S. city?

 A: The world's largest fish! The Georgia Aquarium is the only place in North America where you can see a whale shark.

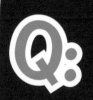 **Q:** Are there professional sports teams in Atlanta?

A: Absolutely! Teams include the Braves (baseball), Falcons (football), Hawks (men's basketball), Dream (women's basketball), and Thrashers (hockey).

 Q: What's one thing every kid should know about Atlanta?

 A: Although it started as a railroad hub, Atlanta is now home to the world's busiest airport.

Atlanta is home to The Center for Puppetry Arts—the largest puppetry museum in North America. Who wouldn't love a Jim Henson puppet?

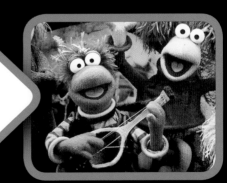

Atlanta... By The Numbers

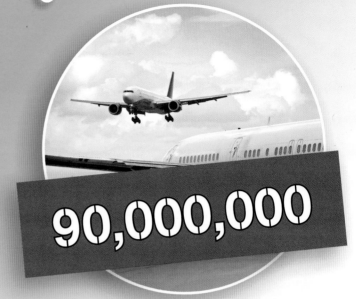

90,000,000

Around 90 million people move through the Hartsfield-Jackson International Airport each year. This means a lot of planes are on the runway. But the action doesn't stop there. An underground "people mover" system shuttles more than 200,000 people around the airport each day!

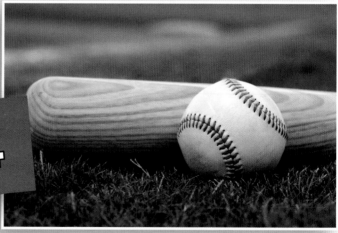

1974

On April 8 of that year, Hank Aaron of the Atlanta Braves hit his 715th home run to break Babe Ruth's record. Hank Aaron remained the major leagues' all-time leading home run hitter for the next three decades.

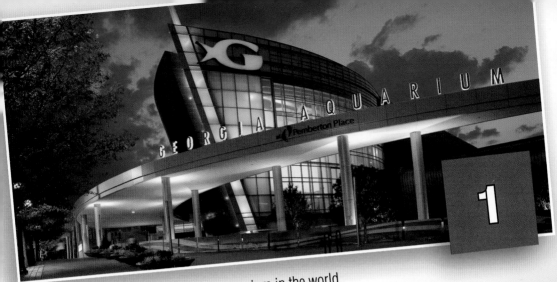

The Georgia Aquarium is the largest aquarium in the world.

5,000,000

Around five million people live in the metropolitan Atlanta area.

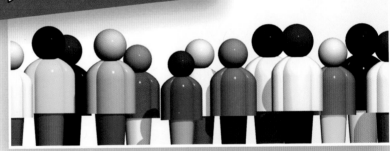

More Numbers!

189	The number of acres in Atlanta's Piedmont Park.
28	The number of counties that make up metropolitan Atlanta.
5	The number of pennies it took to buy a glass of Coca-Cola in 1886, the year Dr. John Pemberton (of Atlanta) invented it.

Atlanta:
Sights and Sounds

Hear

...the music, sound effects, and splashing water at the Fountain of Rings in Centennial Park. The park was built when Atlanta hosted the 1996 Summer Olympics.

Taste

...Georgia's freshest fruits and vegetables at the Atlanta State Farmers' Market, which is considered to be one of the largest of its kind in the world.

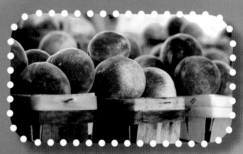

...a lychee-flavored soft drink—or dozens of other different flavors from around the globe—at the World of Coca-Cola.

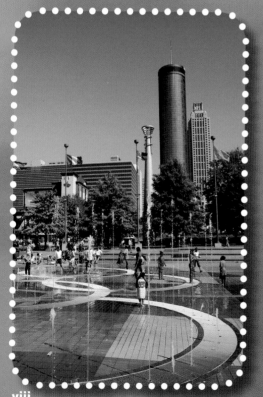

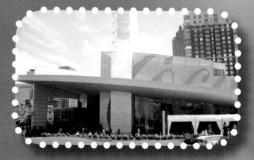

See

… giant pandas at Zoo Atlanta! Research done at the zoo helps scientists learn more about how we can help these rare animals survive.

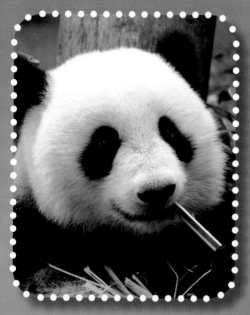

…the world's largest laser light show (including spectacular fireworks!) at Stone Mountain Park.

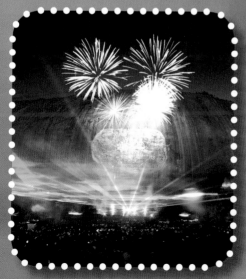

Explore

… the Martin Luther King Jr. National Historic Site. It includes the birthplace, childhood home, and grave site of this important American civil rights leader.

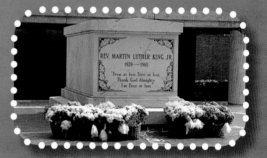

…the grounds around the Capitol. The dome is covered with a thin layer of real gold that was mined at Dahlonega, Georgia.

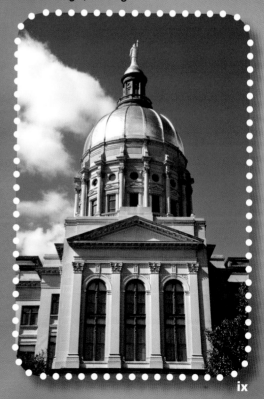

STRANGE BUT TRUE!

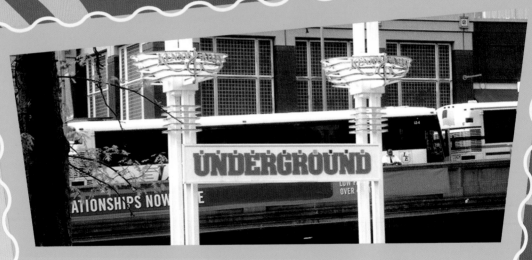

A CITY BENEATH A CITY

The five-block area of Underground Atlanta sits one level below some of the city's newer streets. During the 1920s, city planners built an elevated, or higher, street system to improve traffic flow. So storekeepers moved their businesses up to the second floor. In the 1960s, the lower levels of these buildings were rediscovered. Underground Atlanta was born.

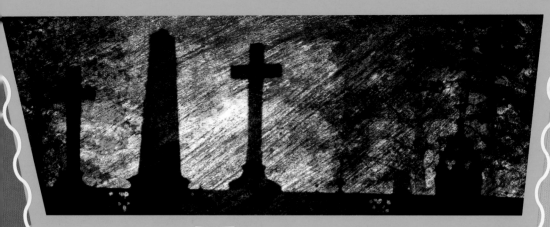

GHOST TOURS

Some tours in the city take people to places where ghosts are supposed to appear. Since the city is more than 170 years old, there are lots of long-ago residents with many interesting stories. Are there really ghosts in Atlanta? You be the judge!

WHICH PEACHTREE?

One of the country's largest 10k races—the AJC Peachtree Road Race—is named after the main north-south street that runs through Atlanta. But if you want to watch, make sure you know where you are going. There are more than 50 other streets, avenues, roads, and drives in Atlanta that also contain the name Peachtree!

Atlanta: Marvelous Monikers

What's a moniker? It's another word for a name...and Atlanta has plenty of interesting monikers around town!

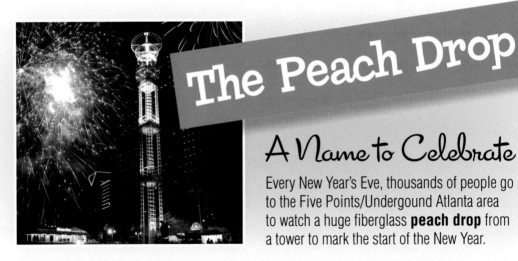

The Peach Drop

A Name to Celebrate

Every New Year's Eve, thousands of people go to the Five Points/Undergound Atlanta area to watch a huge fiberglass **peach drop** from a tower to mark the start of the New Year.

A Famous Name

Just three letters—**CNN**—spell one of the biggest names in broadcasting. The CNN Center is in the heart of downtown Atlanta.

The CNN Center

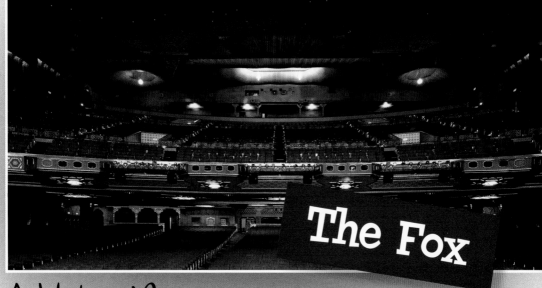

The Fox

A Historic Name

The Fox Theater has been entertaining people in Atlanta for decades and was named a National Historic Landmark in 1976.

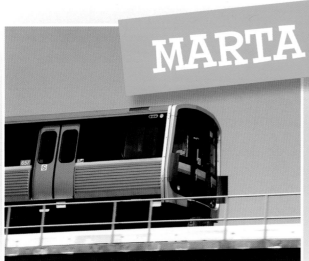

MARTA

A Moving Name

The Metropolitan Atlanta Rapid Transit Authority is a citywide rail and bus system that carries people all over the city. **MARTA** even allows people to bring their bikes on the trains.

The Big Peach

Many Names

Atlanta had lots of previous official and unofficial names: Terminus, Thrasherville, and Marthasville. And don't forget the popular nicknames: **The Big Peach** and Hotlanta!

Atlanta:
DRAMATIC
DAYS

A HARSH
Order!

On September 7, 1864, Union General William T. Sherman ordered that munitions factories, railroad yards, mills, and other targets that could be useful to the Confederacy be destroyed. Fires were lit and spread throughout the whole city. Atlanta was left in ruins.

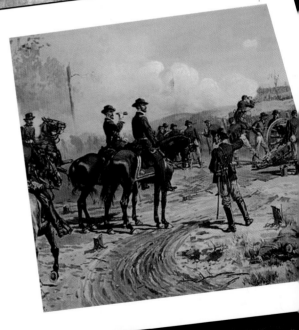

A FRIGID *Storm!*

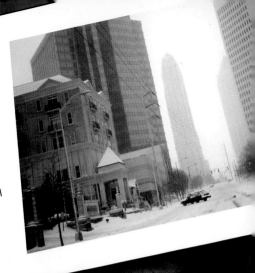

Atlanta rarely sees significant snow, but in mid-March of 1993, the city was paralyzed by a blizzard. Traffic on Interstate 75 was backed up for 80 miles from Atlanta to the Tennessee border!

A HUGE *Celebration!*

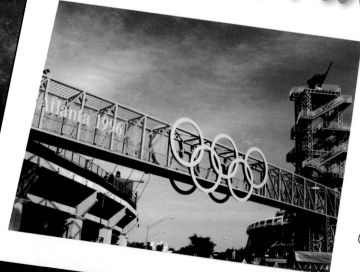

The Celebration of the Century—That's the motto of the Centennial Olympic Games hosted by Atlanta in the summer of 1996. Muhammad Ali ended the Olympic Torch Relay and lit the flame in the stadium where 80,000 people cheered to open 16 days of Olympic competition.

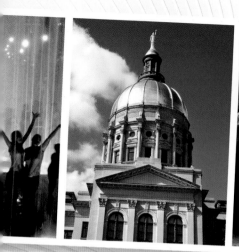
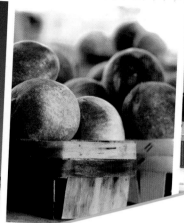
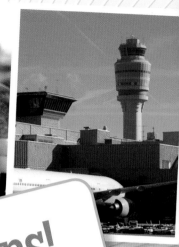

Congratulations!

You have just completed a kid-sized tour of Atlanta... but there's more to explore!

The city of Atlanta is an important part of the state of Georgia. Why? It's because the city helps shape the state and the state helps shape the city!

Read on to find out more...

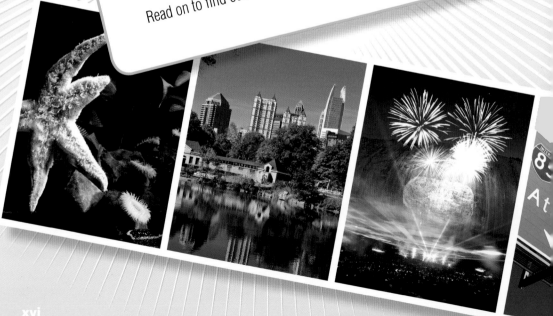

Georgia

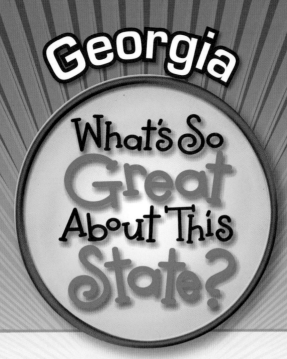

What's So Great About This State?

There is a lot to see and celebrate...just take a look!

CONTENTS

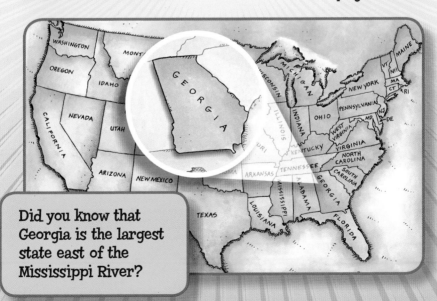

Did you know that Georgia is the largest state east of the Mississippi River?

Well, how about...
the land!

From the Mountains...

You won't get bored when you travel around the state of Georgia! Why? The state has five (yes, five!) different regions. Each region has landforms, plants, and animals that make it special.

The very northern part of the state has mountains, valleys, and plateaus. Thick forests and cool lakes are in this region. Water twists and turns through rivers like the wild Chattooga. But soon the tall mountains give way to the rolling hills of the Piedmont region. This is where most of the state's biggest cities are found.

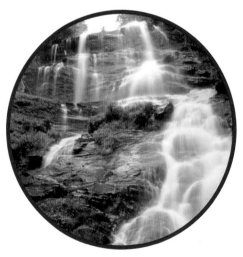

One of the tallest waterfalls east of the Mississippi River can be found in northern Georgia's Amicalola Falls State Park.

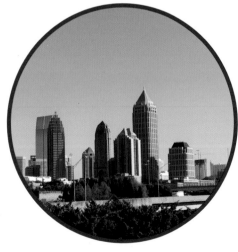

Atlanta, the capital city of Georgia, is located in the Piedmont region.

...To the Ocean

Keep on traveling south and you will find the Coastal Plains. This region makes up more than half the state. The upper part of this region has great soil. So this is where the tasty "P" crops grow. What are they? Peanuts, peaches, and pecans, of course!

The lower part of the Coastal Plains gets…well, lower! This means marshes and swamps begin to appear. Keep going south and east to find sandy beaches. That's right! The eastern part of Georgia has the Atlantic Ocean as its border.

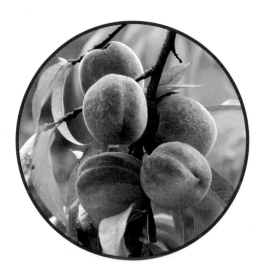

Soil in the Coastal Plains grows tasty peaches.

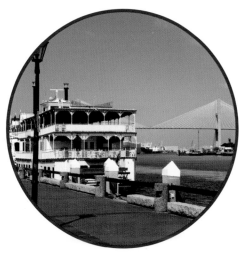

The Savannah River flows past the city of Savannah toward the Atlantic Ocean.

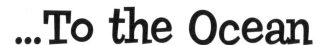

Pine trees in a southern Georgia swamp

Mountains, Valleys, and Plateaus

BLUE RIDGE

RIDGE AND VALLEY

APPALACHIAN PLATEAU

Blue Ridge Mountain Range in northern Georgia

Do you like high places? Then visit the northern part of Georgia. It has three regions: the Blue Ridge Mountains, the Ridge and Valley region, and the Appalachian Plateau.

What's up in the Blue Ridge region?

Just about everything! After all, this northeastern area of the state is part of the Blue Ridge Mountain range. Brasstown Bald—the highest point in Georgia—is here.

A hike through the Blue Ridge region is a back-to-nature treat. Water rushes over waterfalls. Thick forests hide black bears, turkeys, and whitetail deer.

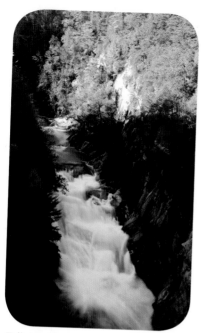

Tallulah Gorge State Park is in the Blue Ridge region.

What can I see in the Ridge and Valley region?

Lots of trees line the sides of the steep ridges. But there's good soil in many of the valleys. You can also find fossils of ancient fish here. Millions of years ago, the area was completely covered in water!

The Ridge and Valley region makes up most of the northwestern part of the state.

...except for that little Plateau region!

There's a tiny region in the far northwest part of Georgia with a big name. It's called the Appalachian Plateau. (A plateau is a high, level area.) One of the flat-topped mountains that form this plateau is called Lookout Mountain.

It's so long it stretches into the neighboring states of Alabama and Tennessee!

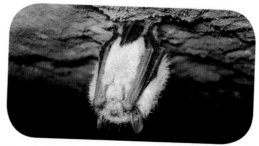

Bats hang out in the many caves found in northwest Georgia.

5

Piedmont and Coastal Plains

The famous Masters Golf Tournament is in the Piedmont region in Augusta, Georgia.

The mountains of north Georgia slowly give way to the hilly area of the Piedmont. Below the Piedmont are the Coastal Plains with flatlands, marshes, and swamps.

What's so special about the Piedmont region?

Well, it has lots of trees. Short-leaf and loblolly pines are in this region. So are oak, hickory, and many other trees.

The Piedmont also has hard rock called granite. The grandest example of granite is at Stone Mountain. This mountain is two miles long and a mile wide.

The Piedmont region ends at the Fall Line. The Fall Line is not a real line, of course. It's just an area where the fast-moving rivers of the Piedmont "fall" onto the lower land of the Coastal Plains.

What can I see in the Coastal Plains?

The largest swamp in the United States! The Okefenokee covers 700 square miles and stretches from southeastern Georgia into northern Florida. Okefenokee is a Seminole name. It means "land of the trembling earth."

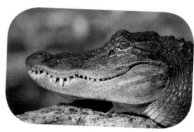

Got gators? The Okefenokee Swamp has plenty!

Why does the land seem to move? Layers of peat moss form on water. Trees and other plants grow in the peat moss. The land looks solid, but it's not. Peat moss can move or cave in. You have to watch your step!

Don't forget the beaches!

To the east the Coastal Plains end in beaches and barrier islands. These are lots of fun—and they protect the land along the coast.

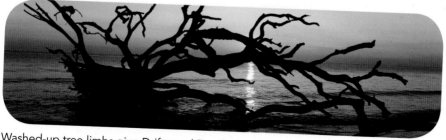

Washed-up tree limbs give Driftwood Beach on Jekyll Island a spooky look at sunrise.

Rivers and Lakes

The Flint River in Sprewell Bluff State Park

Water flows through all the regions of Georgia. The state has thousands of miles of rivers and lots of lakes, both big and little.

Why are the lakes and rivers so special?

Lakes and rivers provide recreation, transportation, food, and habitats! Some of the lakes in Georgia weren't formed by nature but are man-made. Lake Lanier is an example. It has over 600 miles of shoreline. That's a lot of space for fishing, boating, and camping.

What can I see at the lakes and rivers?

Striped bass, rainbow trout, and bluegill! These are just some of the colorful fish swimming in Georgia's lakes and rivers.

Border lines

Some of the rivers in Georgia have a special job. They form borders with other states.

The Chattooga, Tugaloo, and Savannah Rivers each share part of the border with South Carolina. On the other side of the state, the Chattahoochee River forms part of the border between Georgia and Alabama.

The St. Mary's River forms part of the boundary between Georgia and Florida. It's a blackwater river. Why? Tons of leaves and other plant parts fall into the river to rot. Stuff (called tannins) from this rotting plant material makes the river water look dark.

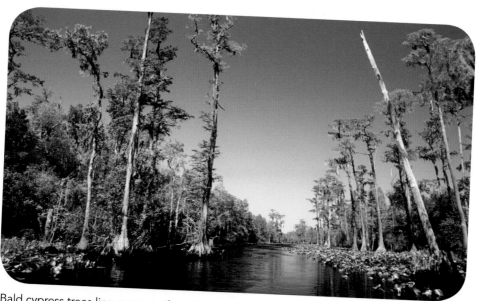

Bald cypress trees line canoe trails in this blackwater river in the Okefenokee National Wildlife Refuge.

Well, how about...
the history!

Tell Me a Story!

The story of Georgia began thousands of years ago. At that time, many Native Americans made their homes throughout the state.

By the 18th century, the Creeks and the Cherokee were the largest Native American groups in Georgia. Spanish explorers had come to Georgia. But James Oglethorpe, a British doctor, settled the colony of Georgia in 1733. He was able to do this with the help of many Native Americans. Tomochichi, the chief of a small Yamacraw tribe, became Oglethorpe's friend and helped him build the city of Savannah. A woman named Mary Musgrove had a Creek mother and an English father. Since she could speak both languages, she helped leaders on both sides keep the peace.

This statue in Calhoun honors Sequoyah. He created the first Cherokee language alphabet. In 1838, the Cherokee were forced out of Georgia. The thousand-mile journey to Oklahoma cost many lives. It is now remembered as the "Trail of Tears."

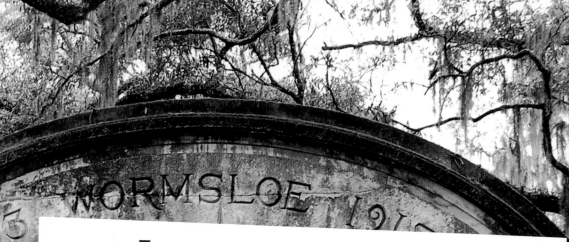

...The Story Continues

Eventually, Georgia became home to many other groups, including European American settlers and African Americans. Many battles for independence were fought in Georgia. Civil War battles, in particular, caused great struggle and loss.

But history isn't always about war. Georgians have always been educators and inventors. They have painted, written, sung, and built. Many footprints are stamped into the soul of Georgia's history. And you can see proof of this all over the state!

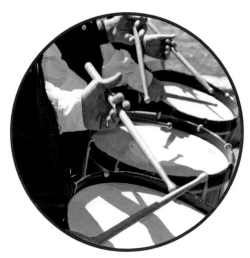

Georgia was the last of the 13 original British colonies. The state had a strong presence in the Revolutionary War.

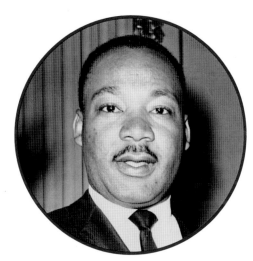

Dr. Martin Luther King Jr. was a civil rights leader born in Atlanta. He received the Nobel Peace Prize for his work.

Wormsloe Plantation in Savannah, Georgia

Monuments

Fort King George Historic Site in Darien, Georgia

Monuments and historic sites honor special people and events. The Fort King George Historic Site helps people remember the first English settlement on the coast of Georgia.

Why are Georgia monuments so special?

That's an easy one! There were many special people who helped build the state of Georgia. Some were famous soldiers and politicians. Others were just ordinary people who did special things to shape the state of Georgia—and the nation.

What kind of monuments can I see in Georgia?

There are many different kinds. From statues to bridges, almost every town has found some way to honor a historic person or event. Even street signs often show the name of someone special.

Where are monuments placed?

Anywhere! The images of three Confederate leaders who served in the Civil War are carved into the side of Stone Mountain near Atlanta.

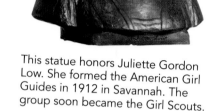

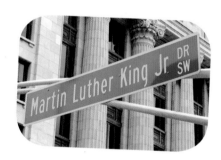

This statue honors Juliette Gordon Low. She formed the American Girl Guides in 1912 in Savannah. The group soon became the Girl Scouts.

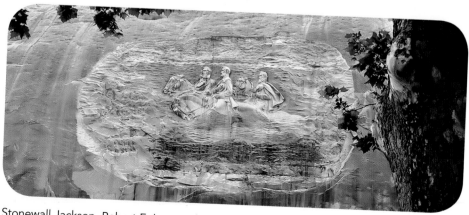

Stonewall Jackson, Robert E. Lee, and Jefferson Davis are carved in the rock at Stone Mountain Park in Stone Mountain, Georgia.

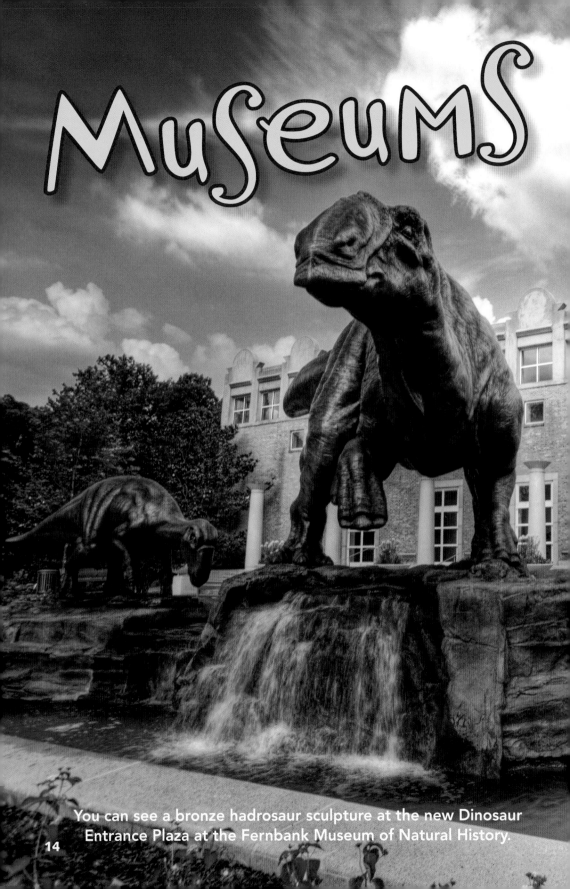

MUSEUMS

You can see a bronze hadrosaur sculpture at the new Dinosaur
Entrance Plaza at the Fernbank Museum of Natural History.

Museums don't just tell you about history—they show you things! How? Artifacts, of course! Museum artifacts are objects or models of objects. Either way, they make history come alive!

Why are Georgia's museums so special?

Amazing museum exhibits tell the story of the state. The Tybee Island Light Station tells a 270-year-old story. General Oglethorpe (the founder of Georgia) decided to build a tall mark to help sailors find the mouth of the Savannah River. So the first lighthouse was built on Tybee in 1736. But due to storms and other damage, two more lighthouses have been built and replaced. The lighthouse that shines on Tybee now is the fourth one built on the island!

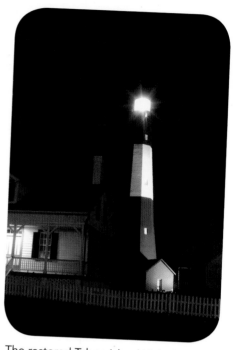

The restored Tybee Island Light Station has 178 stairs.

What can I see in a museum?

An easier question to answer might be "What can't I see in a museum?" There are thousands of items in different museums across the state. Do you want to know about home run hitter Henry "Hank" Aaron? The Georgia Sports Hall of Fame and Museum in Macon, Georgia, is loaded with sports stories. Or maybe you'd like to know more about the 39th President of the United States. Then the Jimmy Carter Library and Museum in Atlanta is the place you'll want to see.

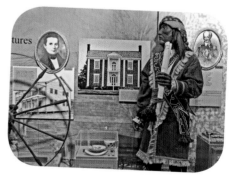

Learn the history of Georgia's Cherokee Nation at the New Echota Historical Site in Calhoun, Georgia.

Plantations

The Brick House on the Calloway Plantation was completed in 1869.

The Brick House on the Calloway Plantation was made from the same kind of red Georgia clay that it stands on. The house is in its nearly original condition. What does that mean? No plumbing, no electricity, no heating, and no air conditioning!

Why are plantations special? (...and what is a plantation, anyway?)

Plantations were large estates or farms. Crops such as rice and cotton were grown on plantations. Enslaved Africans, and, later, enslaved African Americans, did most of the work on a plantation.

Today, many plantations tell the shared history of our country. All have interesting stories of race, families, and sacrifice.

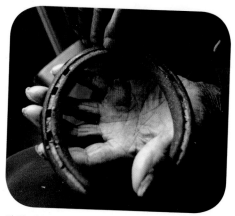

Skilled blacksmiths made horseshoes on plantations.

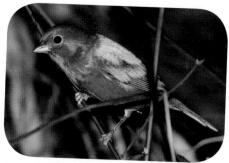

You can see more than plantations on the Colonial Coast Birding Trail! More than 300 different kinds of birds have been spotted along this trail. The painted bunting is one of them.

What can I see if I visit a plantation?

Georgia has plenty of antebellum plantations. Antebellum means "before the war." Which war? The American Civil War that was fought from 1861 to 1865.

Many antebellum plantations show you what life was like 150 years ago. Some showcase the work of enslaved people who became skilled workers. Other plantations have been changed and brought up to date. Now an old plantation might also be a new hotel.

...and there's more!

Cotton grew well on plantations in the southern and middle parts of Georgia. But rice was the crop to plant along the coast. You can see some of these rice plantations when you travel the 100-mile-long Colonial Coast Birding Trail.

Well, how about...
the people!

Enjoying the Outdoors

More than nine million people call Georgia their home. So it should be no surprise that there are lots of different viewpoints in the state. Yet Georgians still rally together to form a very friendly group. They are known for their Southern hospitality. This helps explain why 50 million tourists visit the state each year!

A mild climate in Georgia allows people to enjoy the outdoors all year round. Fishing, boating, hiking, swimming—the list of things that Georgians like to do goes on and on!

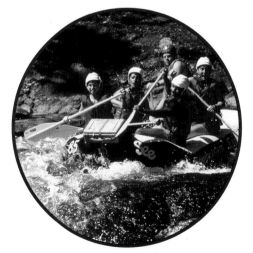

Whitewater rafting on the Chattooga River is lots of fun!

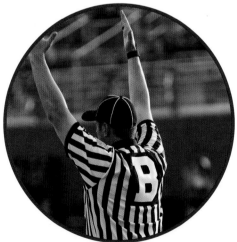

Football stadiums swell with fans to watch any Georgia team!

Sharing Traditions

The people of Georgia celebrate many different heritages and traditions. The Gullah culture is one example. It was formed by enslaved people who were brought to Georgia. A combination of English and African words developed into a special Gullah language. This Gullah language and culture is still celebrated today—especially on the barrier islands off the coast of Georgia.

Did you ever wonder what a Civil War battle was like? Georgians often re-create battles from different wars to honor the memory of brave soldiers. Cooking is another way to pass on traditions. Great Southern food recipes are cherished family keepsakes!

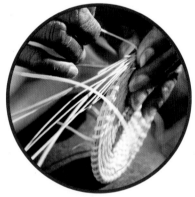

Weaving sweetgrass baskets is one Gullah tradition that has become a well-respected art.

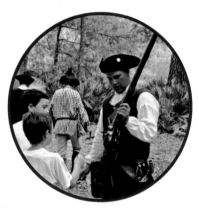

You can see reenactments of battles that were fought long ago at the Wormsloe Historic Site in Savannah.

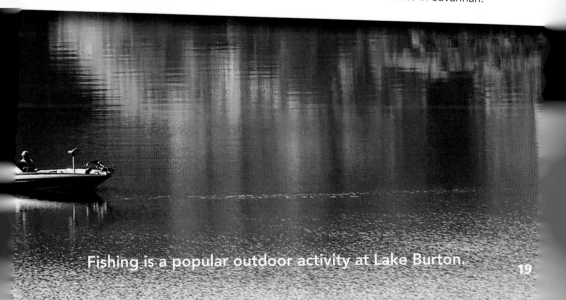

Fishing is a popular outdoor activity at Lake Burton.

Protecting

The Georgia Aquarium in Atlanta is the world's largest indoor aquarium. Aquatic animal conservation and research are among its major goals.

Protecting Georgia's natural resources is a full-time job for many people!

Why is it important to protect Georgia's natural resources?

The many different environments in Georgia help shape its character. In the rugged northeast, tall cliffs stand guard over fast-moving rivers in the Tallulah Gorge. As you move south, rolling hills, red clay, and farmland cover more than half the state. Finally, marshes and blackwater rivers give way to miles of beaches along the coast and barrier islands. All these different environments provide habitats for the many different plants and animals in the state. That's called biodiversity—and it keeps the environments balanced and healthy.

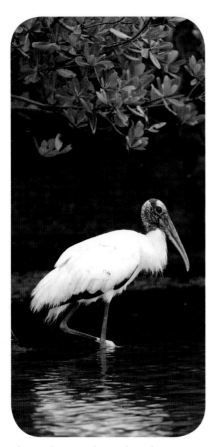

Who protects these resources?

It takes a lot of groups to cover it all. The U.S. Fish and Wildlife Service is a national organization. The Georgia Department of Natural Resources and the Georgia State Parks Service are state organizations. Many smaller groups exist as well.

And don't forget...

You can make a difference, too! It's called "environmental stewardship"— and it means you are willing to take personal responsibility to help protect Georgia's natural resources. It's a smart choice for a great future!

The endangered wood stork can be found in Georgia.

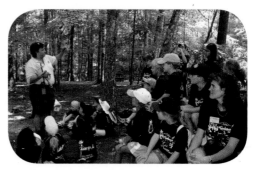

Learn about a forest habitat at Red Top Mountain.

Creating Jobs

Many people work at Atlanta's Hartsfield-Jackson International Airport. It's the busiest airport in the world.

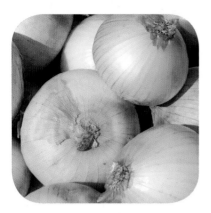

Vidalia onions are a favorite vegetable! They are grown only in southern Georgia.

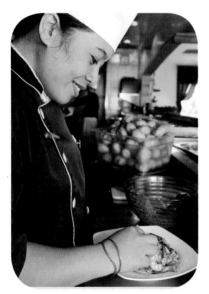

Chefs are needed to prepare food for the tourists in Georgia.

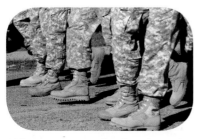

Military training is hard work!

Some jobs have been done in Georgia for a long time. Growing cotton is one of them. Other jobs are newer to the state. These include transportation, medicine, and filmmaking, to name a few.

Why is Georgia a good place to work?

Great natural resources and great people! These two things help businesses grow.

What kinds of jobs are available throughout the state?

Farming is big. Cotton, peaches, pecans, peanuts, and onions are just some of the crops grown in Georgia. The many trees in Georgia also support a large timber industry.

The transportation industry provides many jobs, too. Think of all the people it takes to move 90 million people through Atlanta's airport each year!

Manufacturing, or making things, is common. Another big industry is the service industry. Many jobs are needed to help tourists sightsee, eat, and relax!

Don't forget the military!

The Air Force, Army, Marines, Navy, and Coast Guard can all be found in the state. Georgians have a great respect for all the brave men and women who serve our country.

celebrating

A Ferris Wheel lights the night
at the North Georgia State Fair.

The people of Georgia work hard. But they also know how to have fun. Georgians celebrate at two state fairs each year! The Georgia State Fair is in Macon. The North Georgia State Fair is in Marietta.

Why are Georgia festivals and celebrations special?

Celebrations and festivals bring people together. Some celebrate music and cooking. Others celebrate arts and crafts. All celebrate the people of Georgia and their talents.

What kind of celebrations and festivals are held in Georgia?

Too many to count! But one thing is for sure. You can find a celebration for just about anything you want to do.

Do you like to eat barbecue? Teams compete in a cook-off for the best barbecue at the National Barbecue Festival in Douglas, Georgia.

Would you rather dance and listen to music? You can do both at the La Fiesta del Pueblo in Tifton, Georgia. This festival celebrates Hispanic culture in southern Georgia.

You can even celebrate on the water! Shrimp boats turn into beautiful floats for the Blessing of the Fleet festival in Darien, Georgia.

Don't forget about the Mud Pit Belly Flop Contest!

Yes, it's true! This contest is just one of the very entertaining events at the Redneck Games in East Dublin, Georgia.

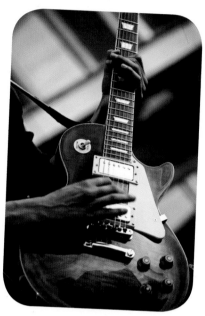

You can hear great jazz at the Music Festival in Savannah.

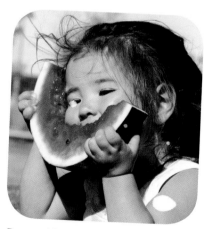

Do you like watermelon? There is always plenty to enjoy at the Watermelon Days Festival in Cordele, Georgia.

Birds and Words

What do all the people of Georgia have in common? These symbols represent the state's shared history and natural resources.

State Bird
Brown Thrasher

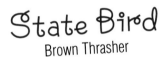

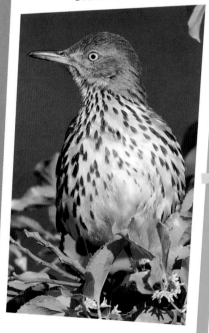

State Flower
Cherokee Rose

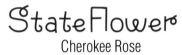

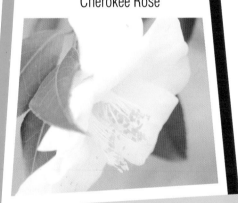

State Tree
Live Oak

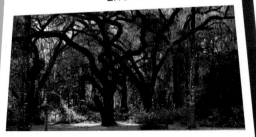

State Fruit
Peach

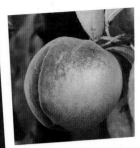

Peaches are also the state fruit of South Carolina and Alabama! However, the state that produces the most peaches in the United States is California!

State Flag
Adopted 2003

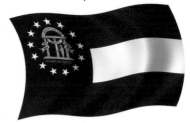

State Reptile
Gopher Tortoise

Gopher Tortoise burrows can provide homes to more than 350 other species of animals!

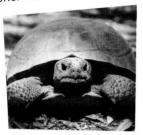

State Crop
Peanuts

Georgia grows more peanuts than any other state!

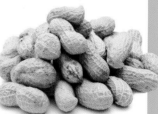

State Insect
Honeybee

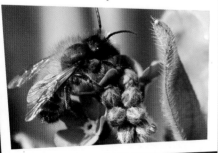

State Butterfly
Tiger Swallowtail

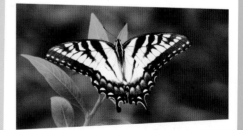

Want More?

Statehood—January 2, 1788
State Capital—Atlanta
State Nickname—Peach State
State Song—"Georgia on My Mind"
State Game Bird—Bobwhite quail

State Wildflower—Azalea
State Fish—Largemouth bass
State Amphibian—Green tree frog
State Shell—Knobbed whelk
State Gem—Quartz

More Fun Facts

More

Here's some more interesting stuff about Georgia.

That's BIG!

Because it has an area of more than 58,000 square miles, Georgia is known as the "Empire State of the South."

An Original

Colonized in 1732 by James Edward Oglethorpe, Georgia was the last of the original thirteen English colonies.

Fit For a King

The state of Georgia was named after King George II of Great Britain.

Border Pals

Tennessee and North Carolina are neighbors to the north. In the south, Georgia runs into Florida. To the west of Georgia is Alabama. To the east is the state of South Carolina and the Atlantic Ocean.

Cotton Cleaner

Eli Whitney developed the cotton gin in Georgia in 1793. The machine made cleaning cotton much easier.

Rock the Vote

Georgia was the first state to allow 18-year-olds to vote.

Lights, Camera, Action

Some movies made in Georgia include Forrest Gump, Driving Miss Daisy, and Smokey and the Bandit.

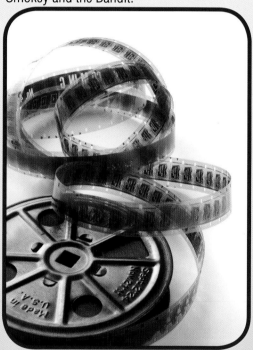

Capital Moves

Before Atlanta took the title in 1868, Georgia had four other capital cities. They included **Savannah** (1733-1786), **Augusta** (1786-1795), **Louisville** (1796-1806), and **Milledgeville** (1807-1868).

A Long Hike
The Appalachian Trail starts in north Georgia and ends in the state of Maine.

Gold Rush
Each fall the small town of **Dahlonega, Georgia** has a festival. It celebrates the discovery of gold in Dahlonega in 1828.

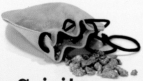

Tree Spirits
Sad faces are carved into some of the oak trees on **St. Simons Island, Georgia**. Many of the faces remind people of sailors who lost their lives at sea.

Famous Fizz
John S. Pemberton invented Coca-Cola in Georgia in 1886. The drink was first sold in a store in **Atlanta**.

A Best Seller
Atlanta native Margaret Mitchell wrote one of the most famous books of all time. *Gone With the Wind* is a story set in the Civil War. It took Ms. Mitchell about ten years to finish the book!

Locals call it "The Forks"
In southern Georgia, the **Oconee** and **Ocmulgee Rivers** become the **Altamaha River** (the largest river in Georgia).

Old School
The University of Georgia at Athens is the oldest public university in the United States The state voted to charter the university in 1785.

Chart Busters
The man who wrote the song "Jingle Bells," James Lord Pierpont, came from **Valdosta, GA**. Ray Charles, a native of **Albany, Georgia** wrote the hit song "Georgia on My Mind."

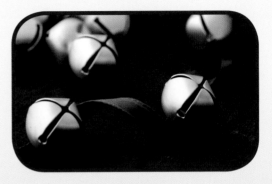

Insect Troubles
Between 1915 and 1923, a little insect made big trouble for cotton farmers. During this time, the boll weevil destroyed more than one third of the cotton crops in Georgia.

A Refreshing River
The **Chattahoochee River** isn't just for fishing and rafting. This river provides drinking water to half the people in Georgia.

A Very Nutty Place
The area around **Albany, Georgia** is known as the "pecan capital of the world" because of the many pecan trees there.

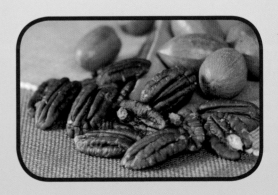

Find Out More

There are many great websites that can give you and your parents more information about all the great things that are going on in the state of Georgia!

State Websites

The Official Website of the State of Georgia
www.ga.gov

Georgia State Parks
www.gastateparks.org

The Official Tourism Site of Georgia
www.exploregeorgia.org

Museums/Albany

Albany Civil Rights Movement Museum
www.albanycivilrightsinstitute.org

Atlanta

Fernbank Museum of Natural History
www.fernbankmuseum.org

The Atlanta History Center
www.atlantahistorycenter.com

Augusta

The Augusta Museum of History
www.augustamuseum.org

The National Science Center's Fort Discovery
www.nscdiscovery.org

Columbus

The Columbus Museum
www.columbusmuseum.com

The National Civil War Naval Museum
www.portcolumbus.org

Rome

Chieftains Museum
www.chieftainsmuseum.org

Savannah

Ships of the Sea Maritime Museum
www.shipsofthesea.org

Savannah History Museum
www.chsgeorgia.org

Aquarium and Zoo/Atlanta

The Georgia Aquarium
www.georgiaaquarium.org

Zoo Atlanta
www.zooatlanta.org

Georgia: At A Glance

State Capital: Atlanta

Georgia Borders: Alabama, Florida, North Carolina, South Carolina, Tennessee, and the Atlantic Ocean

Population: Approximately 9 million

Highest Point: Brasstown Bald at 4,786 feet above sea level

Lowest Point: Sea level on the coastline

Some Major Cities: Atlanta, Augusta, Columbus, Savannah, Athens, Macon, Rome

Some Famous Georgians

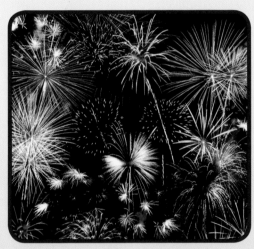

Martin Luther King Jr. (1929–1968) from Atlanta, GA; was a clergyman and leader in the African-American Civil Rights movement.

Gladys Knight (born 1944) from Atlanta, GA; is an award winning R & B singer/songwriter and author.

Juliette Gordon Low (1860–1927) from Savannah, GA; was founder of Girl Scouts of the U.S.A.

Otis Redding (1941–1967) from Dawson, GA; was a grammy winning singer.

Conrad Aiken (1889–1973) from Savannah, GA; was a Pulitzer Prize winning author.

Julia Roberts (born 1967) from Smyrna, GA; is an Academy award winning actress.

James E. Carter, Jr. (born 1924) from Plains, GA; is the 39th President of the United States and Nobel Peace Prize winner for promoting human rights.

Jack "Jackie" Robinson (1919–1972) from Cairo, GA; was the first African American man to play major league baseball with the Brooklyn Dodgers in 1947.

William J. Hardee (1815–1873) from Camden County, GA; was a famous lieutenant general in the Confederate Army.

Alice Walker (born 1944) from Eatonton, GA; is a Pulitzer Prize winning author.

Trisha Yearwood (born 1964) from Monticello, GA; is a grammy winning country singer.

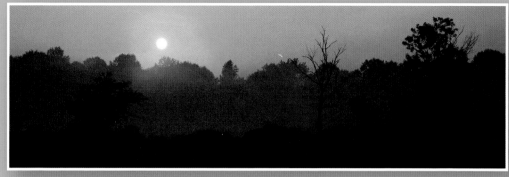

Sunrise over the Chattahoochee River near Roswell, Georgia.

CREDITS

Series Concept and Development
Kate Boehm Jerome

Design
Steve Curtis Design, Inc. (www.SCDchicago.com); Roger Radke, Todd Nossek

Reviewers and Contributors
Neville Bhada, Southeast Tourism Society; Mary L. Heaton, copy editor; Eric Nyquist, researcher

Photography
Back Cover(a), 27d © Alex Staroseltsev/Shutterstock; Back Cover(b), 13c © Greg Henry/Shutterstock; Back Cover(c), 7a © Condor 36/Shutterstock; Back Cover(d), 18a Courtesy Georgia Department of Economic Development; Back Cover(e), 26c © Stacey Lynn Payne/Shutterstock; Cover(a), 3b © Travel Bug/Shutterstock; Cover(b), 2b, 4-5, 13b © Katherine Welles/Shutterstock; Cover(c), 17b, 21a © Bob Blanchard/Shutterstock; Cover(d) © Jeff Kinsey/Shutterstock; Cover(e) © iofoto/Shutterstock; Cover(f), 3a © Tomas Pavelka/Shutterstock; 2-3 © Michael Carlucci/Shutterstock; 2a, 8-9, 12-13, 15b, 19b, 21b © Georgia Department of Natural Resources; 5a © jackweichen_gatech/Shutterstock; 5b © Tom Grundy/Shutterstock; 6-7 Courtesy Mbrooks/Wikimedia; 7b, 18-19, 32 © Sebastien Windal/Shutterstock; 9 Courtesy Ryan Hagerty/U.S. Fish and Wildlife Service; 10-11 © Genevieve Bailey; 10a, 13a © Ed Jackson/University of Georgia; 11a © Lawrence Roberg/Shutterstock; 11b Courtesy Library of Congress; 14-15 © Bryant Upchurch for the Fernbank Museum of Natural History; 15a © Mary Terriberry/Shutterstock; 16-17 © Roger Nance; 17a, 19a © Perry Baker/SCPRT; 18b © Mike Flippo/Shutterstock; 20-21 © Anton Bryksin/Shutterstock; 22-21 © Stephen Finn/Shutterstock; 23a © Lisa Schneider/Shutterstock; 23b © erwinova/Shutterstock; 23c © John Wollwerth/Shutterstock; 24-25 © Michael Sussman; 25a © Pindyurin Vasily/Shutterstock; 25b © Rebecca Abell/Shutterstock; 26a © John A. Anderson/Shutterstock; 26b Rosetta-hidek/Shutterstock; 27a © Margo Harrison/Shutterstock; 27b © Pakmor/Shutterstock; 27c © Rose Thompson/Shutterstock; 27e © PBorowka/Shutterstock; 27f © Leighton Photography & Imaging/Shutterstock; 28 © Terence Mendoza/Shutterstock; 29a © Scott Rothstein/Shutterstock; 29b © Marie C. Fields/Shutterstock; 29c © David P. Smith/Shutterstock; 31 © R. Gino Santa Maria/Shutterstock

Illustration
Back Cover, 1, 4, 6 © Jennifer Thermes/Photodisc/Getty Images

ISBN 978-1-58973-011-3
Library of Congress Catalog Card Number: 2009943361

1 2 3 4 5 6 WPC 15 14 13 12 11 10

Published by Arcadia Publishing
Charleston SC, Chicago IL, Portsmouth NH, San Francisco CA

For all general information contact Arcadia Publishing at:
Telephone 843-853-2070
Fax   843-853-0044
Email   sales@arcadiapublishing.com
For Customer Service and Orders:
Toll Free   1-888-313-2665

Visit us on the Internet at www.arcadiapublishing.com